MAURETANIA

Pride of the Tyne

Ken Smith

Sponsored by Swan Hunter (Tyneside) Ltd.

Newcastle Libraries & Information Service in association with Tyne & Wear Museums

Acknowledgements:

The author wishes to thank the following for their kind help and support: Swan Hunter (Tyneside) Ltd.; Tyne & Wear Archives; Tyne & Wear Museums; *Shipping World and Shipbuilder* magazine; Neil Benson, Executive Editor, Newcastle Chronicle & Journal Ltd.; Dick Keys; Richard Potts, retired principal archivist, Tyne & Wear Archives; David Swan; Norman Gilchrist; Cunard Line; the Cunard Archive, University of Liverpool; the staff of Newcastle City Libraries.

Newcastle Libraries & Information Service gratefully acknowledge Swan Hunter (Tyneside) Ltd. for sponsorship of this book.

Quotations from an *Evening Chronicle* article of 1906 are reproduced by permission of Neil Benson, Executive Editor, Newcastle Chronicle & Journal Ltd. Quotations and photographs from the 1907 *Mauretania* Souvenir Edition of *The Shipbuilder* are reproduced by permission of *Shipping World and Shipbuilder* magazine.

City of Newcastle upon Tyne
Community & Leisure Services Department
Newcastle Libraries & Information Service

ISBN: 1 85795 043 7

Cataloguing-in-Publication Data: a catalogue record for this book is available from the British Library.

Front cover illustration:

The Cunard liner *Mauretania* passing down the River Tyne. (From the Souvenir Edition of *The Shipbuilder*, 1907. The painting shows *Mauretania* in her completed colours, and was based on a photograph taken when *Mauretania* left the Tyne for preliminary trials, September 1907. The artist is not known.)

Back cover illustrations:

The *Mauretania* moves down the Tyne for her delivery voyage to Liverpool, 22 October, 1907.

The *Solitaire* under conversion at Swan Hunter (Tyneside) Ltd., Wallsend, 1997.

The roundel on the title page and the picture of *Mauretania* by moonlight on page 44 are from the 1907 *Mauretania* Souvenir Edition of *The Shipbuilder.*

Cover design by A.V. Flowers.

Also by Ken Smith:

Turbinia: the Story of Charles Parsons and his Ocean Greyhound, Newcastle Libraries & Information Service with Tyne & Wear Museums, 1996.

Printed by Bailes The Printer, Mill House, Market Place, Houghton-le-Spring, Tyne & Wear DH5 8AN

Contents

Page

Photographs

Page

*Turbine power. The **Mauretania** on the measured mile during her official trials in early November 1907 when she achieved a top speed of 27.36 knots with her powerful turbine engines. The trials took place in the Irish Sea and Firth of Clyde.*

~ Injured Pride ~

On 20 September 1906 the Cunard passenger liner *Mauretania* was launched into the River Tyne at the Wallsend Shipyard of Swan Hunter and Wigham Richardson Ltd. Her debut upon the waters of this famed river in North-East England marked the birth of a legend. The *Mauretania* was to become an emblem of the pride, skill and energy of Tyneside workmanship.

The four-funnel ship, at 31,938 gross tons the largest liner built on the Tyne, went on to hold the coveted Blue Riband for the fastest crossing of the North Atlantic longer than any other ship and was undoubtedly one of the most successful passenger vessels of her era.

The *Mauretania* was born out of British national pride as much as commercial considerations. Along with her sister, the ill-fated *Lusitania,* she was the United Kingdom's answer to the German liners which had held the Blue Riband during the ten years preceding her maiden voyage in 1907.

Germany had first captured the Atlantic speed record in 1897 with the four-funnel *Kaiser Wilhelm der Grosse* which achieved a speed of 22.35 knots on the eastbound passage in November of that year. Her performance was particularly annoying for patriotic Britons as in 1897 they were celebrating Queen Victoria's Diamond Jubilee, marking the 60th anniversary of her accession to the throne.

In July 1900 the *Deutschland* became the second German liner to win the Blue Riband, clocking up 22.42 knots on the westward passage and 22.46 eastward. A year later she increased her westward speed to 23.06 knots. She was followed in 1902 by the *Kronprinz Wilhelm* (23.09 knots westward) and then in 1904 by the *Kaiser Wilhelm II* (23.12 knots westward). In 1906 the *Kaiser Wilhelm II* also captured the eastward passage record from the *Deutschland* with a speed of 23.58 knots.

Britain's Cunard Line had naturally watched with alarm as German ships dominated the honours upon the Atlantic. Its directors therefore began negotiations with the government of the day on how they could best meet this German challenge.

Cunard was also worried by another threat. It was posed by the huge American-owned International Mercantile Marine Company under J. Pierpont Morgan, which had acquired controlling interests in several Atlantic shipping lines and which in December 1902 added Britain's famed White Star Line to its fast growing empire. Many people were anxious that Cunard should stay a British owned company and were worried that it might be swallowed up by the rapidly growing shipping combine.

In 1903 the government and Cunard agreed that two large, fast passenger ships should be built to win back the Blue Riband for Britain and re-establish her supremacy on the flourishing crossing to New York. Under the terms of the agreement, which was ratified by Parliament, the government agreed to loan Cunard £2.6 million for the building of the two ships. On top of this, it was to grant the company an annual subsidy of £150,000 towards the upkeep of the vessels, which were to carry the mails.

However, important conditions were attached to this financial aid. It was stipulated that the two liners would have to maintain a speed of between 24 and 25 knots in moderate weather and that the ships would be made available as armed auxiliary cruisers in time of war. In addition, Cunard was required to remain a British company and all the ships' officers as well as the majority of their seamen were required to be British.

Directors and managers of C.S. Swan and Hunter Ltd., 1895. Back row, left to right, F.J. Culley, cashier and chief clerk, later joint company secretary; C.S. Swan, director, later Sir Charles Swan; G.B. Hunter, chairman; C. Stephenson, Wallsend Yard manager and former chief draughtsman; E.W. de Rusett, naval architect. Front row, left to right, R.F.W. Hodge; R. Hudson, commercial assistant to G.B. Hunter, later company secretary; A. Claughton.

Swan, Hunter, Stephenson and de Russet all played a leading role in masterminding the creation of ***Mauretania.*** *C.S. Swan was the son of Charles Sheriton Swan, founder of C.S. Swan and Co., owners of the Wallsend Shipyard. The company, which later became C.S. Swan and Hunter Ltd., merged with Wigham Richardson, of the Neptune Shipyard, in 1903 to combine resources to bid for the* ***Mauretania*** *contract. The new company was named Swan, Hunter and Wigham Richardson Ltd.*

(Photo: courtesy of David Swan)

The order for one of the ships, *Mauretania*, was placed with Swan Hunter and Wigham Richardson of Wallsend, and the other, *Lusitania*, with John Brown of Clydebank.

Before work could begin on building the vessels careful planning was needed to ensure as far as possible that they would be the fastest liners upon the prestigious Atlantic run. Cunard therefore appointed a special commission of experts to inquire into what would be the best type of engine to capture the Riband. This was one of the most important considerations of the entire project. The commission was headed by the marine superintendent of Cunard, James Bain, and its members also included Andrew Laing, manager of the Wallsend Slipway and Engineering Co. Ltd.

After a great deal of study, the commission eventually decided that the relatively new turbine engine, the invention of Tyneside engineering genius Charles Parsons, should be chosen. But the decision was something of a gamble. No one knew exactly whether turbines of the power needed to drive such large ships at such great speeds would be successful when put to the test upon the ocean. Turbine engines of 68,000 horsepower, constructed to the designs of Parsons, would be needed to maintain speeds of between 24 and 25 knots as required by the agreement. Machinery of this order had never before been installed in ships.

Two Tyneside companies, C.S. Swan and Hunter, of the Wallsend Shipyard, and Wigham Richardson, of the Neptune Shipyard, Low Walker, merged in 1903 to combine their resources to bid for the *Mauretania* contract. Swan and Hunter was no stranger to Cunard. Its slipways had already seen the launch of two intermediate-sized Cunard passenger liners, the *Ivernia* and *Carpathia*. The standard of its designs and workmanship had clearly impressed the shipping line. The firm resulting from the merger, Swan, Hunter and Wigham Richardson Ltd., was thus by no means an unknown quantity and after submission of various designs it won the lucrative order to build the ship.

The contract for the turbine engines of the *Mauretania* went to the Wallsend Slipway and Engineering Co. Ltd., of Willington Quay, Wallsend. This concern had strong links with Swan, Hunter and Wigham Richardson, and had built the reciprocating engines for the *Ivernia* and *Carpathia*. Now it was to construct the giant turbine machinery of the *Mauretania*, its greatest challenge to date. The management and workforce of Wallsend Slipway and Engineering were to prove highly successful in meeting this challenge. Behind their success, however, stood Charles Parsons, the inventor of the steam turbine engine, whose brilliance and ingenuity were the ultimate reasons for the great liner's speed achievements.

Andrew Laing, manager of the Wallsend Slipway and Engineering Co. Ltd., builders of the ***Mauretania****'s turbine engines.*
(Photo: Shipping World and Shipbuilder)

Under construction at the Wallsend Shipyard. The giant frames of the ***Mauretania.*** *Note the workmen in the interior. This photograph was taken on 4 April 1905.*

The cellular double bottom of the great liner takes shape at Wallsend in May 1905. The framing at the fore end is now completed. The cellular double bottom formed a series of water ballast tanks and gave added protection against damage.

~ Launch of a Legend ~

The builders of the *Mauretania* carried out extensive tests to determine the best form of the ship's hull and other details using a wooden launch 47.5ft long. This model, a one-sixteenth scale replica of the ship's hull, was driven by electric motors. It was thoroughly tested in the Northumberland Dock, Howdon, on the Tyne where the model had a run of about a quarter of a mile. The wooden launch provided valuable information on how the new ship might perform when completed.

The keel of the *Mauretania* was laid down at Swan, Hunter and Wigham Richardson's Wallsend Shipyard in 1904 after a preliminary agreement was initialled by the parties. The following year the main contract was signed and the work got fully underway.

The great liner was built on a berth inside a huge shed constructed of metal girders and posts. This shed was more than 130ft high and over 700ft long. It featured a glazed roof which enabled building to proceed in virtually all weathers and arc lamps were provided to allow work on the berth at night. The roof girders were fitted with electric overhead cranes.

The giant ship which took shape at Wallsend had an overall length of 790ft and a maximum beam of 88ft. She was driven by four huge propellers, each with three and later four blades, linked directly to her turbine engines, which were placed under the waterline. Equipped with twenty-five boilers and 192 coal-burning furnaces, the ship needed 324 firemen and trimmers to

Workmen leaving the vessel during fitting out. This phase took just over a year. The turbines and boilers were lifted into the ship by the floating crane, ***Titan.***

(Photo: Newcastle City Libraries)

Giant propeller. Workmen under one of the four huge propellers. Initially, each of these had three blades. In 1909 the number of blades was increased to four on each propeller and the liner's speed performance improved.

A bow view before the launch. The vessel was constructed inside a 130ft-high shed.

man the stokehold.

Carbon, mild and silicon steels were all incorporated into the hull and superstructure and it was said that around four million rivets were used. The passenger accommodation featured thirty different varieties of woods.

By September 1906 the *Mauretania* was ready for her launch, after which she would be moved by tugs to her fitting-out mooring alongside the yard. Two large dolphins (mooring structures) had been sited in the river for this purpose. Other preparations included special dredging operations to ensure adequate water depth.

The launch ceremony was performed on 20 September by the Dowager Duchess of Roxburghe. Not surprisingly, thousands of onlookers crowded the banks of the Tyne at Wallsend and Hebburn. The shipyard itself was also packed with spectators. They were entertained by the 1st Newcastle Artillery Band.

Christening the ship *Mauretania*, the name for the ancient Roman province of north west Africa, the Dowager Duchess broke a bottle of wine over the liner's bows. As the ship began to move towards the Tyne, steamers sounded their sirens, adding to the cheers of the crowds. She entered the water only forty seconds after starting her journey. The *Mauretania* was born.

There was only one accident reported during the launch. A workman was slightly injured when a piece of glass from the shattered wine bottle fell on his head. However, he was quickly given first aid and was said to be little worse for his experience.

The *Evening Chronicle* sent a 'Special Correspondent' to view the launch from the Ballast Hills at Hebburn on the opposite bank of the river to Wallsend. The reporter found the hills covered with people packed so tightly that he had to struggle to reach the top of one of these mounds.

The correspondent told readers in a colourful account: "Climbing further up, and pushing my way into the throng, an occasional glimpse of the river was secured, and finally, after much floundering and persistent effort, I was rewarded with the view of a lifetime. The whole panorama was laid out underneath one.

"In the centre of the crescent formed by the bend of the river, just opposite was the *Mauretania*, dwarfed by the huge shed, but still an imposing construction with her four white propellers startlingly outlined in the picture. They seemed to adorn the stern like so many ornamental stars. On either side were the yards and factories of mid-Tyne, backed by a streak of green country, while in the front was the river, placid and sunlit, and guarded east and west by a cordon of gaily-decked passenger boats.

"On every stretch of quay, and projection, and structure by the sides of the river were to be seen crowds of human beings all arranged with one object in view, but not all, possibly, well and comfortably placed. The adventurous spirit who climbed to the top of a chimney stack in the neighbourhood of Walker, was surely not comfortable, though he had an excellent bird's eye view. But doubtless every position had its drawbacks and compensations.

"Strange to say, the remarkable feature in connection with this view from the Ballast Hills, was the great silence which reigned over everything. Not a blow or a whistle was heard. The river steamers had banked their fires, people coughed as though they were in church, no one talked. Everyone was anxiously waiting.

"Presently, in the extreme stillness, the band playing far away at the back of the yard on the other side could be faintly heard. Then the blows

Ready for the water. A view of the elegantly-shaped stern. Her four propellers "seemed to adorn the stern like so many ornamental stars", wrote a reporter.

All set and smart. The official launch party assemble in front of the giant liner's bow on 20 September 1906. Soon the great ship would enter the Tyne. The top guests included the First Lord of the Admiralty, Lord Tweedmouth, William Watson, Chairman of Cunard, and the Hon. Charles Parsons and his daughter, Rachel. The numbers painted on the bow are draught marks to indicate the ship's level in the water.

of the carpenters as they knocked out the chocks seemed to be an accompaniment to the music.

"A muffled cheer next came over the water, and someone whispered 'She is coming'. It was a false alarm. One gentleman ventured to dwell on the likelihood of her sticking fast, and breaking her back, but the crowd would not listen. They quietly and fixedly kept their eyes on the vessel whose stern was adorned with the four white stars. 'It is just like a Sunday' remarked one gentleman, who, having only one eye, had exactly half the trouble of looking for the launch and just so much more time to be talkative. Smokers knocked out the ashes of their pipes just as dogs during an eclipse drop the bones they have been worrying.

"In ten minutes or more the crowd seemed spellbound. Enterprising spectators ceased to push or scramble for better stands; everybody was waiting silently. And then at last the great vessel was seen to move. The motion was seen even before the cheering and the screeching of sirens had travelled across the water, and almost at once the hill of silence broke out into convulsions of excitement.

"In contrast with all this wild shouting and cheering the great vessel glided gently and noiselessly into the water. She took her floating level so easily, and with so little commotion, except that caused by the general fanfare, that standing on the hill one almost could have imagined it was a fine moving picture thrown upon the screen.

"The first impression of the great vessel was that she stood abnormally high out of the water in proportion to her length, but as the tugs got hold of her stern and swung her starboard bows into line the beautiful and noble proportions of the vessel became most apparent. People viewed the long, splendidly modelled steamer with admiration, and they did well to make the most of their brief opportunity, for within a very few minutes the volumes of smoke from the now moving steamers almost completely hid her from view. Truly she had found her birthplace in the smoky Tyne!"

Some of the smoke was coming from the six tugs which towed the *Mauretania* to her nearby fitting-out mooring where

The launch. The ship moves down the ways at Wallsend on 20 September 1906. The ceremony was performed by the Dowager Duchess of Roxburghe. All went well according to plan, except for a minor accident involving a workman.

(Photo: Newcastle City Libraries)

Waterborne at last! The ship with the knife-edged bow enters the water. Her entry into the Tyne was slowed by 1,000 tons of drag chains. "People viewed the long splendidly modelled steamer with admiration," commented an ***Evening Chronicle*** *correspondent.*

(Photo: Newcastle City Libraries)

she would receive her funnels, engines, and boilers and where work on her cabins, public rooms and a host of other details would be carried out.

The fitting-out of the liner took just over one year and represented a tremendous feat of labour by the workers of the Wallsend Shipyard. The boilers and other heavy machinery, including the six turbines, were lowered into the ship by a large floating crane, the *Titan*, capable of lifting 150 tons.

On 17 September 1907, as the vessel neared completion, she was taken down the Tyne to the North Sea for preliminary trials which lasted five days. Large crowds flocked to the river's banks to see the *Mauretania* put to sea for the first time. On her journey down river she was towed and guided by the Dutch tugs *Ocean* and *Poolzee* and the South Shields tugs *Snowdon* and *Washington.*

During her test runs the liner's speed performance was encouraging. She achieved a maximum of 27.75 knots and averaged over 26 knots while steaming between St Abb's Head in Berwickshire and Flamborough Head, Yorkshire. Carrier pigeons were released from the ship to take news of the progress of the trials to the Wallsend Shipyard.

On 21 September the vessel returned to the Tyne. A month later all was ready. The *Mauretania* had taken two years, five months to build from the signing of the full contract in 1905. At the date of her completion she was the largest ship of any description to be launched on the river, and the liner was truly the pride of Tyneside. An army of Geordie workmen had poured all their energy and skill into her creation.

It must have been a proud occasion for them when the ship was thrown open to the public for viewing on 12 October. Those who wished to look around the vessel paid two shillings and sixpence and the proceeds went to local charities.

On the afternoon of 22 October 1907 the great ship departed the river of her birth for delivery to Cunard in Liverpool and for her official trials. Tens of thousands of cheering people crowded the Tyne's banks as the tugs *Snowdon*, *President*, *Washington* and *Gauntlet* moved and guided her down to the open sea. The passage took eighty minutes and all went smoothly.

In her element. A fine bow view of the ***Mauretania*** *in mid-river immediately after her launch. "The beautiful and noble proportions of the vessel became most apparent".*

The sirens of the many small boats and the hooters of shipyards and engine works sounded out a salute to the huge vessel. As she left the river those who waved her farewell could not have realised that this four-funnel queen from Wallsend was on course for a career of unparalled success.

*Paddle tugs attend to the **Mauretania** after the launch. Soon the fitting out of the 790-ft-long ship would begin.*

The ***Mauretania*** *leaving the Tyne for her preliminary trials in September 1907. News of the trials' progress was taken to the Wallsend shipyard by carrier pigeon.*

(Photo: Newcastle City Libraries)

A splendid atmospheric view on the afternoon of October 22 1907 as the newly completed ***Mauretania*** *moves down the Tyne, escorted by tugs, to begin her delivery voyage to Liverpool. She sailed northwards around Scotland to reach her destination. Among those aboard was the Chairman of Swan Hunter & Wigham Richardson, George B. Hunter.*

(Photo: Newcastle City Libraries)

~ The Supreme Ship ~

The *Mauretania* steamed northwards around Scotland on her delivery voyage. She was in no rush but still managed an average speed of 22 knots. Among those aboard for the trip were the chairman of Swan, Hunter and Wigham Richardson, George B. Hunter, the manager of Wallsend Slipway and Engineering, Andrew Laing, and a host of other figures connected with the Tyneside shipbuilding world.

The liner reached the Canada Dock, Liverpool, on the morning of 24 October. Before her maiden voyage, however, she had to undergo her official trials, which took place in the Irish Sea and the Firth of Clyde during early November.

In the Irish Sea, she was tested on four long runs, two southwards and two northwards, between Corswall Point Light on the south west coast of Scotland and the Longships Light, off Land's End, a distance of 304 nautical miles. On one run she achieved an impressive 27.36 knots and her average speed for all four runs was 26.04 knots.

The second trial took place on the measured mile off Skelmorlie in the Firth of Clyde where the liner clocked up 26.75 knots. Afterwards, runs were made in the Firth between Holy Isle and Ailsa Craig on which she achieved a mean speed of 26.17 knots. The ship had therefore proved conclusively to Cunard that she was capable of meeting the rate of knots required of her.

The *Mauretania* left Liverpool on her maiden voyage to New York on the evening of November 16 1907. She was

An unusual stern view in dry dock, probably at Liverpool. Policemen keep watch over the dock area. Before World War I the ship's home port was Liverpool. Afterwards, she was switched to Southampton.

Chief Engineer John Currie. He was in charge of the ***Mauretania****'s engines from 1907 to early 1910, the period in which she established herself as the fastest transatlantic liner.*

(Photo: Shipping World and Shipbuilder)

Captain John Pritchard. He commanded the ship on her delivery voyage from the Tyne to Liverpool and on her maiden voyage to New York in the autumn of 1907.

(Photo: Shipping World and Shipbuilder)

under the command of Captain John Pritchard and at that date was the world's largest liner. A cheering crowd of about 50,000 people turned out in wet weather to watch her depart from the Prince's Landing Stage.

Steaming into the night down the Irish Sea, she encountered calm conditions and the following morning reached Queenstown (Cobh), where she took aboard more passengers and mails. She left the Irish port after a two-hour call and glided away into the vast expanse of the North Atlantic.

However, it was not long before the ship was to experience her first taste of that ocean's immense power. The liner started to run into the teeth of a westerly gale and soon the winds had reached 50mph. Her bows rose and fell steeply as she met the giant waves head on. Tons of water came crashing on to her foredeck and a spare anchor broke loose. The ship slowed to a mere three knots and her bows were turned away from the wind to enable crewmen, at great risk to themselves, to secure the anchor again. Throughout this procedure she was being violently buffeted by the storm.

Resuming her course, the *Mauretania* made good headway

Majestic four-stacker. The ***Mauretania*** *at sea. The ship's prominent cowl ventilators distinguished her from her sister,* ***Lusitania,*** *whose ventilators were of much lower profile. Tragically,* ***Lusitania*** *was torpedoed by a U-boat in 1915 and sank with the loss of 1,198 lives.* *(Photo: Newcastle City Libraries)*

despite the rough seas and on the afternoon of the following day conditions began to moderate a little. The damage caused by the storm included broken promenade deck windows, bent railings and water-stained carpets. In defiance of the bad weather, it seemed that she still might achieve a record crossing. Her engines and the men who drove them had performed admirably.

But it was not to be. Fog as well as the storm robbed her of the Blue Riband on her maiden passage westward. This was encountered off Sandy Hook in the approaches to New York. The ship was forced to anchor amid the murk. To proceed further would have been highly dangerous considering the large amount of shipping in the area.

Within hours, however, the fog rapidly lifted and the *Mauretania* docked in New York after a crossing lasting five days, 18 hours and 17 minutes. Her speed had averaged between 21 and 22 knots.

On 30 November the ship departed New York on her

homeward passage to Liverpool. Fog was again encountered, this time off the Newfoundland Grand Banks, but after a little over a day it cleared and the liner picked up speed, her turbines and stokers working flat out to achieve a record. And this time the *Mauretania* carried off what was then the most glittering prize of the seas. She captured the Blue Riband for the eastward crossing with an average speed of 23.69 knots. The passage from the Ambrose Light, New York, to Queenstown, Ireland, had taken four days, 22 hours, 29 minutes.

Ironically, *Mauretania* had wrested the eastward record from her Clyde-built sister, *Lusitania*, rather than a German ship. The *Lusitania* had entered service a month earlier and on her second voyage had captured the Riband from the Germans for both westward and eastward crossings. Now, she was forced to give up the eastward honour to the ship that was the pride of the Tyne. More significantly, however, between them the two British liners now held the record for both directions and had been the first passenger ships to cross the Atlantic in under five days.

In the next few years there followed a friendly contest between the sisters as they vied against each other for the honours. *Mauretania* first gained the westward record in May 1908, steaming across at an average 24.86 knots. But in July of that year *Lusitania* won the westward record back (25.01 knots). However, she never regained the eastward honour from her sister.

Also in 1908, one of *Mauretania*'s propellers was damaged,

The "Mauretania" is

Practically Unsinkable

Owing to the Watertight Bulkhead Doors being
Hydraulically controlled by

THE STONE-LLOYD SYSTEM.

Echoes of the ***Titanic****? An advertisement from the Souvenir edition of* ***The Shipbuilder****. Under five years later similar claims of near 'unsinkability' were made by some people about the ill-fated* ***Titanic,*** *though her watertight doors were not to blame for the disaster which befell her when she struck an iceberg in April 1912. A deficiency in the design of the watertight compartments themselves was a major factor in the tragedy. The* ***Mauretania,*** *when first commissioned, carried only sixteen lifeboats.*

suffering the loss of a blade. Cunard decided to have a new set of propellers fitted, this time with four instead of three blades. The new screws made their debut in early 1909 and considerably improved her performance.

The decisive moment came in September 1909 when *Mauretania* re-took the westward honour, achieving an average of 26.06 knots between Daunt's Rock and Sandy Hook. The passage had taken four days, 10 hours, 51 minutes. She was now the champion in both directions and from that date onwards *Mauretania* reigned as the supreme ship. She held on to the Blue Riband for a record length of time, retaining the eastward honour for 22 years and the westward for 20.

In September 1910, exactly a year after recapturing the westward prize, she again clocked up 26.06 knots on the passage to New York. This time she clipped ten minutes off her own time, crossing in four days, 10 hours, 41 minutes. Steaming in the same direction in January the following year, she averaged 27.04 knots during a day's run.

Soon, her fame was spreading on both sides of the Atlantic. Between early 1909 and late 1911 she made eighty-eight crossings of the Atlantic without undergoing a refit. On most of these runs the ship averaged over 25 knots.

During this period of sustained hard work she also gained a reputation for the reliability of her arrival and departure times. Passengers who travelled aboard her developed a fond affection for the fast and elegant ship from the Tyne which moved through the waves with a grace and dignity few could fail to admire.

The mooring chains for ***Mauretania.*** *The weight of each end link was 336 lbs. The total weight of the moorings was over 200 tons and the anchors weighed 12 tons each. They were manufactured by Brown, Lenox & Co., Pontypridd.*

(Photo: Shipping World & Shipbuilder)

~ Elegant Queen ~

During her twenty-eight-year lifetime the *Mauretania*'s passengers ranged from millionaire businessmen and famous personalities in the luxurious first-class accommodation to poor emigrants in her plain third class bound westward to seek a better life in the New World. However, in 1922 the United States introduced strict quota limitations on the number of immigrants allowed to enter the country and this naturally led to a steep drop in this type of passenger. The answer was a new 'tourist' class, an attempt to attract those of moderate income who might wish to travel for pleasure rather than business or necessity.

When she entered service, the liner could carry 560 passengers in first-class, 475 in second class and 1,300 in third. Her crew numbered 812. The vessel could thus accommodate more than 3,000 people.

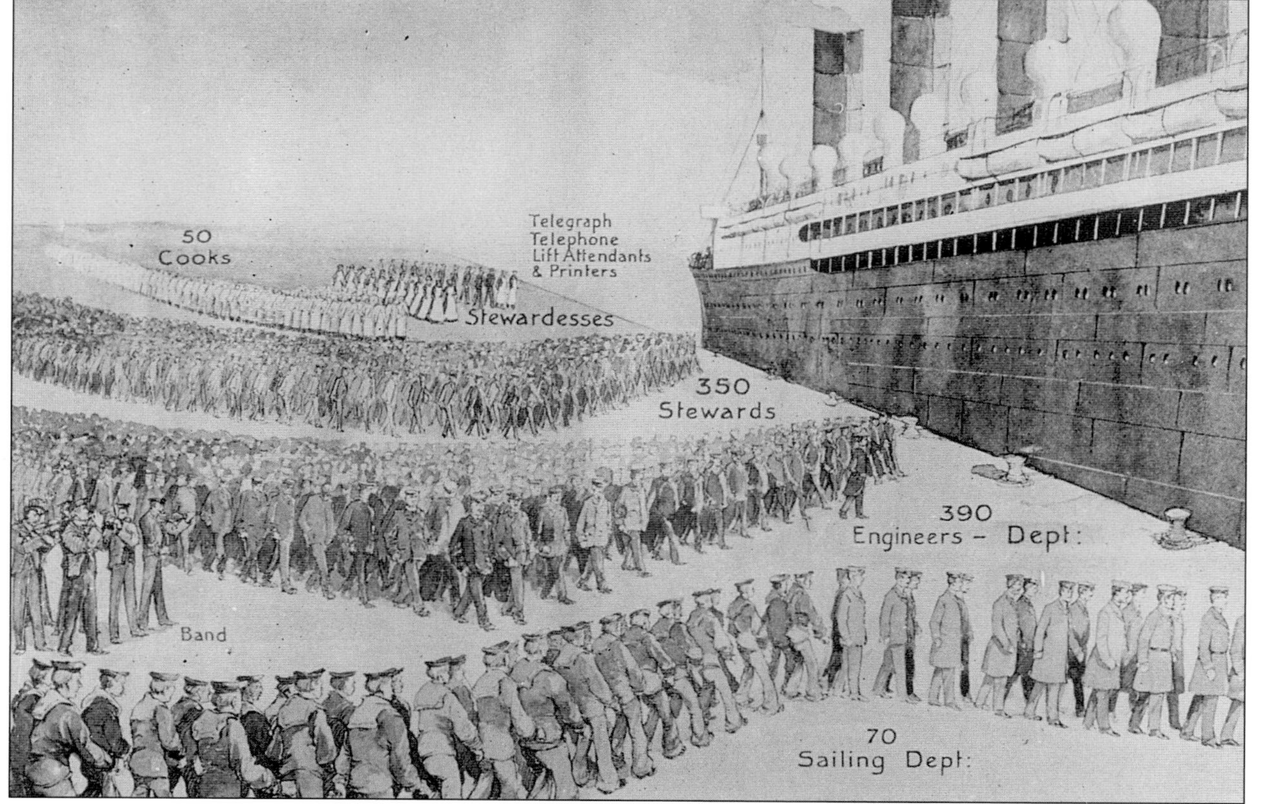

Many hands. An artist's view of the crew of the ***Mauretania.*** *They numbered over 800.*

The first-class areas of the ship included beautifully decorated public rooms and luxury private staterooms, all containing a wealth of woodwork panelling and elegant furniture. These sumptuous interiors were designed by Harold Peto, who had previously gained a fine reputation for his country house interiors. Much of the decoration was in the styles of the Italian and French Renaissance of the 15th and 16th centuries. A large amount of the woodwork for the interiors was manufactured in the joinery department of the Wallsend Shipyard.

The November 1907 souvenir number of *The Shipbuilder* magazine, celebrating the completion of the ship, commented on Peto's designs and the skilled work of the joinery department: "The whole effect is rich and interesting, and may fairly be described as a triumph for all concerned."

The first-class accommodation was sited amidships, being spread over five decks. These were connected by a grand staircase and other staircases as well as two electric lifts. *The Shipbuilder* told readers of the grand staircase and entrances: "The woodwork is French walnut, the panels being veneered with some of the finest figured wood that one could wish to see." The magazine singled out the grand staircase for particular praise: "The grand staircase is unequalled in size and beauty in any vessel afloat, and indeed it is worthy of any mansion ashore." The carpet on the stairs was "of a delightful shade in green, serving to accentuate the beauty of the panelling". Recesses in two of the entrances contained long seats featuring carved woodwork.

Luxury. A first class special stateroom on D deck. Fine woods of several varieties and comfortable furnishings were used in cabins of this class, giving a "home from home" feeling for rich passengers.

The first-class dining saloon was situated on two storeys, surmounted overall by a dome. Both the upper and lower dining levels were panelled in straw-coloured oak in the style of the French king, Francis I. They featured fine individual carvings cut back from the face of the solid wood. The interior of the dome was adorned with the signs of the Zodiac. The colours used were as rich as the ornamentation. Upholstery was deep pink throughout and the carpet of the lower saloon cerise red. The dining areas could seat a total of 480 passengers.

The first-class lounge, also known as the music room, was in 18th century French style. Describing the room as a "noble apartment" and "charming", *The Shipbuilder* declared in admiration: "It is difficult at first to realise that one is afloat when in this beautifully-shaped room, with its rows of stately columns and its graceful semi-circular bays; and only those who know how a designer is hampered by the position of

Elegance. A view of the upper and lower levels of the first class dining room, surmounted by a magnificent dome. The upholstery was in deep pink.

funnels, ventilators, beams, girders and the various necessities of the modern ship, can properly appreciate the ingenuity displayed."

The panelling, columns and pilasters of the lounge were of mahogany. The wood was polished a rich golden brown, with gilt mouldings and carvings. Also featured, were sixteen pilasters of marble, cream curtains with coloured borders and three fine French tapestry panels. The furniture included chairs and sofas of polished beech covered in brocades of varying colours.

The lounge was crowned with an oval dome. *The Shipbuilder* again commented enthusiastically: "The oval dome of wrought iron with gilt ornaments, and the plainly panelled white ceiling from which are suspended crystal electroliers, complete a room unequalled in any steamship and rarely surpassed even in a palace."

The library and writing room contained sycamore panelling stained a silver grey. Also in 18th century style, mouldings were again gilt, but the gold was given a greenish tint which was intended to be in harmony with the panelling. Along one side of the room was a huge bookcase with delicately carved wooden doors. Carpets and curtains were coloured a deep rose and the seats, made partly from mahogany, also featured this colour.

The style of the first-class smoking room was 15th century Italian. Its richly carved panels were combined with an inlaid sycamore border. Recesses contained divans and card tables. Windows in the recesses featured arches reminiscent of those in a mansion or luxury hotel.

The *Mauretania*'s first-class public areas also contained a new feature which was soon to be repeated in other ships. For the first time afloat, a "Verandah Café" was one of the amenities provided. Situated on the boat deck, the café was described by *The Shipbuilder* as "one of the many delightful innovations" of the vessel. The magazine painted an attractive picture of its pleasant situation: "Here passengers may sit and sip their coffee in the open air, perfectly protected from the weather. Evergreens have been trailed along the glazed roof, giving the passenger an impression of shore comforts."

Also included for the sons and daughters of first-class passengers was a children's room. Here, the panelling was decorated with paintings by the artist J.E. Mitchell, of Newcastle. They illustrated the nursery rhyme *Four and Twenty Blackbirds*. Special dining tables and seats were provided for the children. The room even featured a large rocking horse.

Two "regal suites" were the *Mauretania*'s most expensive

private cabins. Each suite contained a drawing room, dining room, two bedrooms, a bathroom and corridor. The drawing and dining rooms of one of the suites were panelled in East India satinwood and fitted with marble mantelpieces. Wall panels were decorated with green silk and heating was provided by electric radiators. Furniture in the Georgian-style bedrooms was made from mahogany. The other regal suite was similar in decoration, although a rose colour was used instead of green.

In addition to these superb private rooms, there were sixty-eight special state and en suite rooms for other wealthy travellers, as well as 109 first-class staterooms. The special state and en suite rooms were also elegantly furnished, featuring a wide variety of fine woods. Many of them had washstands of onyx marble.

Plants and informality. The Verandah Café, one of the first afloat. "Here passengers may sit and sip their coffee in the open air, perfectly protected from the weather," reported ***The Shipbuilder.*** *This picture was taken before full furnishings and decorations were added.*

The second-class accommodation was said to equal the first for comfort but not for magnificence. However, the decoration of the public rooms was still of great beauty and elegance. The second-class dining saloon was Georgian in style and decorated with oakwood. Here, as in first class, a dome was also provided as part of the effect. An electric ornamental light (electrolier) was suspended from the centre of the dome. Facing each other at opposite ends of the room were a large carved oak sideboard and a piano. With its parquet flooring, on which were laid green runners, this dining saloon was indeed impressive.

The second-class drawing room contained maple wood and gilt adornments in French 18th century style. It was crowned by yet another dome, this time of obscured glass with a gilded metal framework. Chairs and sofas were upholstered

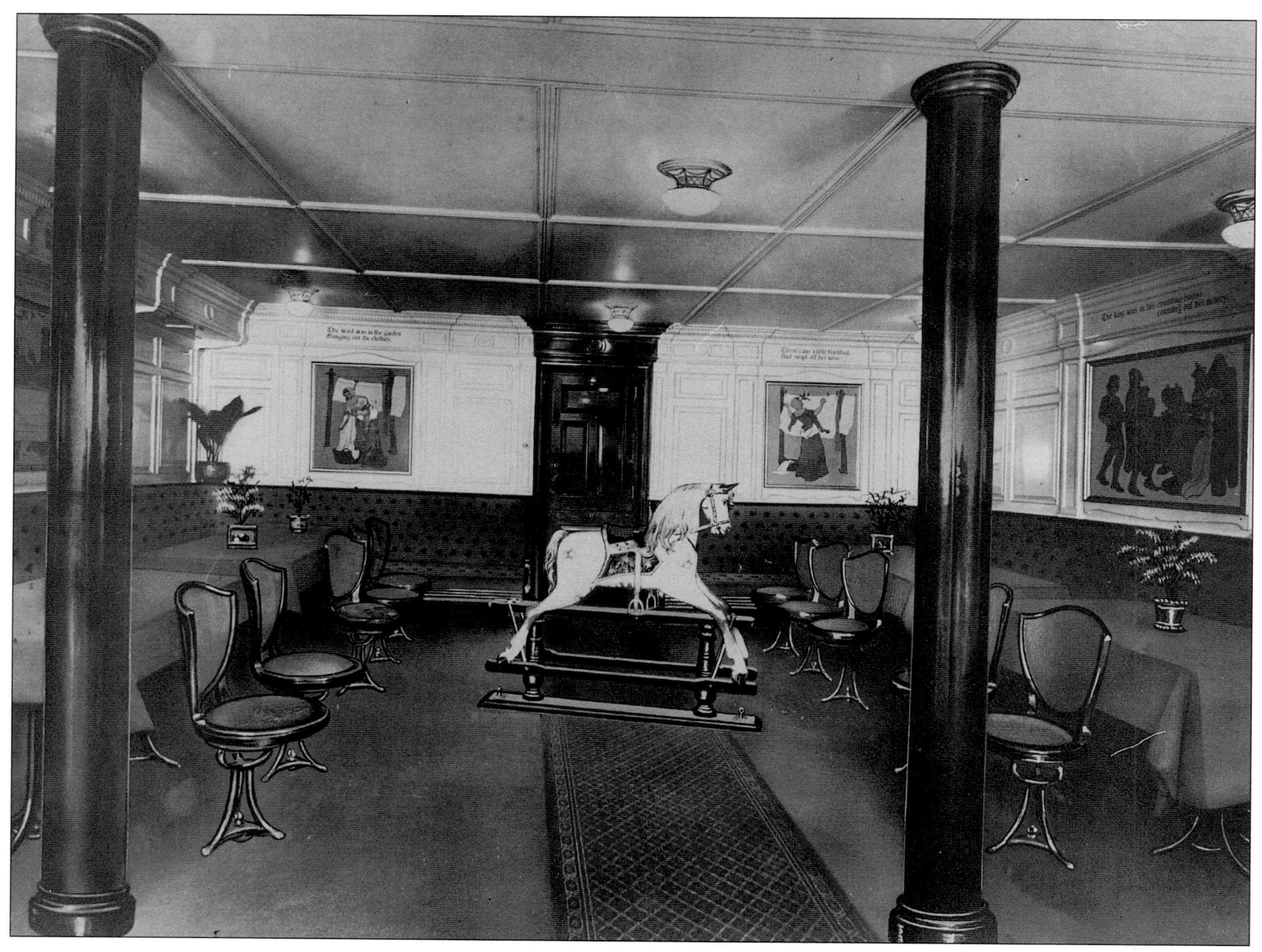

The children's room aboard the liner, complete with rocking horse. The nursery rhyme pictures on the theme of 'Four and Twenty Blackbirds' were by the artist J.E. Mitchell of Newcastle.

A section of the first class lounge or music room showing a tapestry panel. Crowned by an oval dome, the room featured panelling, columns and pilasters of mahogany.

Spartan. A host of chairs in the third-class general room. The contrast with first-class public rooms could hardly be greater. Class distinction reigned on sea as on land in Edwardian times. The minimum third class one way fare before World War I was around £6 to £7.

in crimson velvet. In the late Georgian-style smoking room mahogany and boxwood were used. Upholstery was a deep blue velvet. The lounge in second class was formed from an extension of the grand entrance on the boat deck. Here, teak was used to provide a good effect. Blue carpet runners were laid on the wood deck and the upholstery was in a colour which matched the carpets. Most of the second-class staterooms were panelled in white with mahogany furniture.

Third-class accommodation was, not surprisingly, much more spartan. In the dining saloon, which extended the full width of the ship, 330 people could eat at one sitting on long bench-like tables with revolving chairs. *The Shipbuilder* described the room as giving "a light and airy appearance". The panelling was of polished ash with teak mouldings. This saloon also contained a piano. The other third-class public areas included a smoking room and ladies' room in the same materials.

The division of the passenger accommodation into three classes very much reflected the rigid class structure of Edwardian society. The wealthy and powerful lived in a different world aboard ship to the poor, mirroring their respective positions ashore. The toilets for first-class passengers on the *Mauretania* were labelled "Ladies" and "Gentlemen", in contrast to those in third class which were simply styled "Male" and "Female".

However, within seven years of the *Mauretania*'s maiden voyage a war was to break out which would shake the faith of ordinary men and women in the wisdom of those with wealth and power. Countless men would die fighting for their different countries in this immense tragedy. People's lives would be altered beyond measure. *Mauretania*'s life would also be changed by the conflict and she would take on unexpected roles far removed from those of a "floating hotel".

Expensive. A drawing room in one of the two ultra luxury Regal Suites. Each suite comprised a drawing room, dining room, two bedrooms, a bathroom and corridor. They were the most expensive accommodation aboard, the fare in such lavish style costing around £200 per crossing.

Between rich and poor. A second class special stateroom. These cabins were mainly panelled in white with mahogany furniture. A second class crossing cost about £10 in the ship's early years.

~ Troops and Nurses ~

When the First World War broke out in August 1914 the *Mauretania* was on her way to New York from Liverpool. But before reaching her destination she received orders to dock at the Canadian port of Halifax, Nova Scotia, instead. There followed three more voyages to Halifax and then she was requisitioned by the Admiralty for war service. This move had been expected since the agreement between Cunard and the government in 1903 had stated that she would be available for use as an armed auxiliary cruiser should a war break out.

However, she was never used as a cruiser. Events soon proved that this was too dangerous a role for such a large and prestigious target as a passenger liner which was particularly vulnerable to attack while coaling. The sinking of two German liners fitted out as auxiliary cruisers in 1914 had convinced the Admiralty that such vessels were unsuitable as warships. The *Mauretania* was therefore laid up and it seemed that she would spend the entire conflict without any useful role.

But the launch of the disastrous Gallipoli campaign in 1915 brought the *Mauretania* an opportunity to prove herself. She was fitted out as a troopship and during three voyages in May, July and August of that year she carried over 10,000 soldiers to the Greek island of Lemnos in the Aegean. From Lemnos the troops would embark in other vessels to the shores of Turkey's Gallipoli peninsula where they would face one of the most terrible situations of the First World War and where many would be killed or wounded in a tragic campaign of utter futility.

These trooping voyages were not without risk to the *Mauretania*. Enemy submarines were always a potential threat. Indeed, while in the Aegean she survived a torpedo attack by a narrow margin. Luckily, her commander at the time, Captain Daniel Dow, spotted the track of the metal 'fish' moving towards his ship. Immediately, he gave the order for the ship to be turned away at all possible speed. It is said that the torpedo missed her by a mere 5ft. The liner then steamed rapidly onwards.

Another event in 1915 brought home to people the great dangers posed by enemy submarines and also illustrated how lucky the liner had been in avoiding disaster. While the *Mauretania* was engaged in embarking Gallipoli-bound troops on the first of her voyages, her sister, *Lusitania*, met a tragic end on a homeward run from New York. She was torpedoed by a U-boat off Ireland's Old Head of Kinsale on 7 May and sank with the loss of 1,198 lives. The attack outraged public opinion in both Britain and America. Now only one of the beautiful sisters was left.

Mauretania's trooping runs to Lemnos were followed by another change of role. In September 1915, work began on converting her into a Red Cross hospital ship. Her task would be to treat and bring home soldiers wounded at Gallipoli. Indeed, it is likely that many of the injured men she carried back to Britain had also travelled to Lemnos aboard her. The conversion to a hospital ship involved her public rooms becoming wards. They were equipped with swing cots for the comfort of the wounded who were attended by a full staff of nurses and doctors. Her hull and superstructure were painted white, and on her sides she bore huge red crosses and a green band, signalling to the enemy that she was engaged on humane and peaceful missions.

The liner accommodated her patients as high up in the ship as possible. The lower areas were considered unsuitable

*The troopship. The **Mauretania** in her dazzlepaint livery. She carried British, American and Canadian soldiers during her wartime service, which also included a spell as a hospital ship during the Gallipoli campaign. Towards the end of the war she bore the name HMS **Tuber Rose.***

since in the event of an emergency it would be more difficult for the wounded to reach the lifeboats.

Under the command of Captain Arthur Rostron, the ship made three voyages to the island of Mudros to embark the wounded, in October, November and December 1915. She landed the men safely in Southampton. In all, *Mauretania* transported home more than 6,000 injured troops. Her complement of nurses and doctors were also returned safely to Britain.

After her three voyages as a floating hospital, the *Mauretania* returned to her role of troopship, carrying more than 6,000 Canadian soldiers on two trips from Halifax to Liverpool in 1916. On one of these voyages she developed serious leaks and the sea poured into her boiler rooms. The water had flooded in via coal ports which had not been sealed with sufficient tightness. For a while the ship took on a list and she was only saved by the determined efforts of her crew who carried out pumping operations and stopped the leaks in difficult conditions.

The great ship thus lived on to experience new phases in her wartime career. Following the Canadian trips, she was laid up near the mouth of the Clyde. She remained there throughout 1917.

The following year she was brought back into service by the Admiralty, this time as an armed troopship. Her task was to carry thousands of American soldiers to Britain, from where they would leave for the Western Front. With Captain Rostron in command, the liner made seven of these trooping voyages from New York to Liverpool in 1918. Flying the White Ensign of the Royal Navy, she was painted in a harlequin-like camouflage livery and given an escort of destroyers. Her name was changed to HMS *Tuber Rose*.

While travelling westward on the last of these voyages, in November 1918, the guns in Europe fell silent. The Armistice had come into effect. *Mauretania* landed the troops she was carrying in Liverpool as required, even though the war had ended. These were lucky men. It was not long before they boarded her again, bound back across the Atlantic.

In the next few months the ship also ferried thousands of other American troops home. They came to love the liner that took them back to safety and peace and nicknamed her the 'Maury'.

The ship had proved herself of great use to the Allied powers during wartime, even though she was expensive to keep on the seas. She emerged from those years of conflict without damage. Most importantly, she had survived a period of extreme danger in which so many other ships had fallen victim to U-boats or mines.

The boat deck promenade with smoke pouring from funnels. Some of the sixteen lifeboats can be seen on the left.

~ The Grand Old Lady ~

In May 1919 the *Mauretania* finished her government service ferrying troops home and was restored to her pre-war condition, her woodwork and furnishings being reinstalled. Improvements were made to cabins and the liner was cleaned and painted. However, her engines did not receive a major overhaul and this was soon to show up in her speed performance.

The ship's home port was switched to Southampton, but with her destination remaining New York. Calls were made at Cherbourg on the way.

Departing Southampton for the first time on 6 March 1920 she averaged just over 21 knots westward. The following month her speed was down to 17.81 knots in the same direction and in May of that year 18.35 knots. For the proud 'Maury', these figures were disappointing. But it was clear that her turbine engines were suffering from the strain and stress of many years' hard work.

It was a fire which finally ended this phase of her career and helped to solve the speed problem. The blaze broke out while she was alongside at Southampton on 25 July 1921, badly damaging first-class cabins amidships and the first-class dining room floor above. Firemen fought the inferno for six hours and succeeded in stopping the blaze spreading to other parts of the ship.

The need to repair the damage prompted Cunard to decide that the *Mauretania* should at the same time be converted to burn oil instead of coal. Accordingly, she was sent back to her builders, Swan, Hunter and Wigham Richardson, of Wallsend, to have the work carried out.

Crowds flocked to the banks of the Tyne to see her arrival in the river of her birth. The task of repairing her and converting her boiler rooms to oil-firing took around six months. In addition, furnishings in the public rooms were modernised, a parquet dance floor was laid in the first-class lounge, more private bathrooms were added to staterooms, new carpets were laid, and many of her private suites were re-panelled in silk.

The *Mauretania* left the Wallsend Shipyard in March 1922 for her return to Southampton. She was towed down the Tyne stern first by the four tugs *Joseph Crosthwaite*, *Ben Ledi*, *Great Emperor* and *Plover*. The tugs *Washington* and *Conqueror* were on station at her bows. But the great liner did not have to suffer the indignity of leaving the river stern first. She was turned off Tyne Dock, her bows now facing seawards.

Later that month, she re-entered service on the Southampton-Cherbourg-New York run and after several more voyages it became clear that the conversion to oil-firing had helped to improve her speed. A number of westward passages in 1922 were accomplished at speeds of 23 and 24 knots, and on one she averaged 25. On the eastward passage she achieved 25 knots on four occasions that year. The oil conversion had also brought about another change – it had greatly reduced the number of crew needed in the boiler rooms.

In 1923 the *Mauretania* went on a cruise for the first time in her career. She was chartered by the American Express Company and cruised for several weeks in the Mediterranean, her passengers being mainly millionaires.

Later that year she was sent to a Southampton yard for her turbine engines to be given a major overhaul, but because of a strike the work had to be finished at Cherbourg. As she was being towed across the Channel by tugs she nearly went adrift in rough weather, but the tugs managed to bring her safely into the French port after an extremely difficult crossing. The overhaul was completed in May 1924 and the ship returned to Atlantic service.

The year 1929 was perhaps the most sad in the *Mauretania*'s entire career, yet in another way she proved herself a ship of extraordinary resilience. It was the year in which she lost the Blue Riband to the new German liner *Bremen*.

The two-funnel *Bremen* and her sister ship the *Europa* were built to win back the Atlantic honour for Germany. With her two broad funnels and low, streamlined superstructure, the 51,656-ton *Bremen* was an impressive example of a modern liner. She was equipped with engines of over 100,000 horsepower, as against the *Mauretania*'s 68,000, and she was fitted with a bulbous bow, an innovation which helped to increase her speed. However, Cunard did not sit back when faced with the possibility of losing the honour. Modifications were carried out to the *Mauretania*'s engines to assist her in dealing with this challenge.

The German ship departed Bremerhaven on her maiden passage to New York in July 1929, immediately capturing the Riband for the westward crossing with an average speed of 27.83 knots between Cherbourg and the Ambrose Light. The time taken was four days, 17 hours, 42 minutes. The *Mauretania*'s 26.06 knots record had at last been broken. The *Bremen* went on to take the eastward honour with 27.92 knots. But the *Mauretania*, by this time known as the 'Grand Old Lady of the Atlantic', did not give up without a fight. Leaving Southampton in August, she crossed to New York at an average speed of 26.9 knots. On the eastward run she clocked up an impressive 27.22 knots. The liner had broken her own record in both directions. It was a remarkable achievement for a ship twenty-two years old, but the *Bremen* remained the faster liner.

In her last years, the *Mauretania* was increasingly used as a cruise ship, and returned to the Mediterranean for these leisurely trips each year between 1925 and 1930. In 1931 the liner undertook several popular weekend cruises from New York to Nassau in the Bahamas. These voyages were dubbed the 'Booze Cruises' because many Americans were taking the opportunity to escape prohibition.

From early 1933 until the autumn of 1934 she took passengers on a series of cruises to the West Indies. Her hull was painted white in keeping with her luxury role in a sunny climate. Some called her the 'White Queen'.

But her passenger accommodation had never been fully updated, her relative lack of private bathrooms being a major disadvantage, and Cunard reluctantly made the decision that the 'Grand Old Lady' should be withdrawn from service. Following a cruise to the West Indies, she crossed the Atlantic from New York to Southampton for the last time in September 1934 at an average speed of over 24 knots, still achieving the rate of knots required of her in the agreement reached between the government and Cunard so many years previously.

The ship was then laid up in Southampton until the summer of the following year while Cunard decided her fate. Eventually, it was agreed that she should be sold. In May, her furnishings and fittings were put up for auction. On 1 July 1935 she departed Southampton on her final voyage – to a breaker's yard at Rosyth. It was a sad moment for all who had grown to love the *Mauretania* as the great ship steamed northwards on course for her last destination.

The great liner leaves the mouth of the Tyne after her oil conversion work on 11 March 1922. This photograph was taken from the South Shields side. Now burning oil instead of coal as fuel, she was given a new lease of life. ***Mauretania*** *did not lose the Blue Riband until 1929 when she was beaten by the German liner* ***Bremen.***

(Photo: ***The Shipyard*** *magazine, courtesy of Tyne & Wear Archives)*

~ Farewell to the Tyne ~

On her voyage to Rosyth to be broken up, the liner stopped off the mouth of the Tyne for nearly half an hour to say farewell to the hard-working people who had built her. They had provided her with a sound hull which had withstood the pounding of many Atlantic storms and with superb engines which had proved their worth time and time again. She was the greatest example of the Tyne's shipbuilding and marine engineering skills.

As the liner drew level with the river mouth, rockets were fired from her bridge in salute to her birthplace. Thousands of people had flocked to the seafronts at South Shields, Tynemouth, Cullercoats and Whitley Bay to catch a glimpse of her on her way to the breakers, her masts shortened to allow her to pass under the Forth Bridge. But the crowds were surprised and thrilled when she came to a halt about two miles off the Tyne piers.

Small boats crowded with sightseers went out to greet her. They sounded their sirens in tribute and several aircraft swooped low overhead. The 'flotilla' of craft was augmented by fishing vessels, tugs and the Shields pilot boat. It was a sad but heart-warming occasion.

Flying from the *Mauretania*'s foremast was a 20ft-long blue ribbon, representing the Blue Riband of the Atlantic. Proudly, it bore the message: "1907 to 1929".

The Lord Mayor of Newcastle, Councillor R.S. Dalgliesh, was at the North Shields ferry landing preparing to journey out to the ship when he received the following radio message from her: "Thank you for your greeting. For twenty-eight years I have striven to be a credit to you, and now my day is done. Though I pass on, may Tyneside ever reach out to further and greater triumphs. With pride and affection I greet you. Farewell – *Mauretania*."

The Lord Mayor and his party were then taken out to the ship by the tug *Plover*. The Mayor of South Shields, Councillor J.W. Watson, also made the journey, but in a separate boat. The councillors boarded the liner and chatted for several minutes to her last commander, Captain. A.T. Brown, on the bridge. Then it was time to leave. They re-boarded the *Plover*, the tug which had helped to bring the *Mauretania* into and out of the river during her 1922 oil conversion. The party sang *Auld Lang Syne* as they stood in the tug. Many others in the host of small craft around them joined in the singing and then people aboard the liner also began to sing. There must have been tears in many eyes.

Soon the *Mauretania* was steaming slowly away from the Tyne on the final leg of her final voyage. Boats again sounded their sirens and onlookers waved handkerchiefs until she was out of sight to the north. She was gone.

But the extraordinary *Mauretania* had established herself as a legend in the history of the Atlantic crossing and was not a ship anyone could forget, least of all the people of Tyneside. She will live on in the hearts of Geordies as the proudest achievement of a great shipbuilding river. She will also find a place in the hearts of all who love the splendour of a great ship.

*A view of **Mauretania**'s impressive funnels looking forwards. The funnels, painted in the Cunard red and black colours, were raked (sloped backwards), conveying an image of speed and power that was entirely accurate.*

~ *Mauretania* Facts and Figures ~

Length overall: 790ft

Breadth (maximum): 88ft.

Gross tonnage: 31,938.

Engines: Parsons turbines. Built by the Wallsend Slipway and Engineering Co. Ltd. to the designs of the Hon Charles Parsons. Four propellers.

Speed: Around 25 knots.

Owners: Cunard.

Builders: Swan, Hunter and Wigham Richardson Ltd., Wallsend.

Launched: 20 September, 1906, by Dowager Duchess of Roxburghe at Wallsend Shipyard.

Completed: October 1907. Left Tyne on October 22 1907 for delivery to Cunard in Liverpool and official trials.

Maiden voyage: Departed Liverpool for New York on November 16 1907.

Honours: Blue Riband eastward 1907-1929. Blue Riband westward 1909-1929.

First World War service: Troop and hospital ship.

Fate: Broken up at Rosyth, 1935.